# THE BIG
# WHAT-IF

by David Neufeld
illustrated by Mary Newell DePalma

## MODERN CURRICULUM PRESS
Pearson Learning Group

"Think!" Austin said to himself. The beach was empty. He stood near a live dolphin stranded on the sand. The dolphin's right eye gazed at him. It was a nice eye, friendly even. The dolphin didn't appear to be injured, it just seemed tired from struggling to get back to the water.

"If I leave, you are doomed," he said. *Doomed* was a word from the "what-if" game he and his friends played. What if the North Pole melted and the ocean rose higher and Brooklyn was doomed? What would you do?

Austin was good at "what-if." He always started with whatever was right in front of him.

He looked around, and saw that the tide was still going out. The waves were breaking a hundred feet away. Dolphins needed to stay wet, he knew.

Austin emptied his bucket onto the sand and out spilled his treasures of the day: a watch, a triple-barb hook, a half-dollar coin, the metal shaft from a fishing spear, and some shells.

"I'll be right back," he told the dolphin.

He ran down to the water and ran back with a bucket full of sea water. After seven trips the dolphin's skin was wet again. Austin sat in the sand. "How long can you stay here?" He knew the dolphin didn't understand, but he also knew dolphins were smart and liked to talk to each other.

"How long can *I* stay here?" thought Austin. His mom would be looking for him around suppertime, and that was just two hours away.

In all the times they'd played "what-if" Austin and his friends had never imagined a dolphin might wash ashore on Brighton Beach. No dolphins had been spotted near that community for years, so Austin had never seen one before.

"What are you doing here?" he asked the dolphin. He crawled forward and touched the dolphin's skin, hoping it wasn't injured.

Dark clouds were rolling in.

"Don't get desperate," he told the dolphin.
"If it rains, it will be good for both of us."
Austin imagined catching rain water in
his bucket.

"If there's lightning, it won't be so good, though," he added. He didn't want to imagine what would happen if a terrible storm broke.

A gang of seagulls hovered over the dolphin. "Get!" Austin shouted in a loud and determined voice.

Two of his friends liked to invent "what-ifs" about buzzards. They'd say, "You broke both your legs falling off a horse in the desert. You're desperate. You drank the last of your water hours ago, and the buzzards are circling!"

"Are you okay?" Austin asked the dolphin. He didn't see any cuts or blood, but the dolphin's skin was getting dry again. The water was no closer than before. "We've got a long wait for the tide," Austin said, "even if you're not injured."

Austin's stomach rumbled. He imagined his mom beginning to worry about where he was. Still, he couldn't leave the dolphin. He picked up the bucket and the broken spear shaft and trudged down to get more water. He stuck the shaft in the sand near the water's edge to measure the tide.

"My mom would never call the police first," Austin said out loud. The lights of the nearby apartment buildings were starting to come on. "She'd ask around if anybody saw me first."

Now the spear shaft was partly under water. "Tide's coming up!" he said.

"What if," he began, "I came by this beach on my way home from Marco's house and found you? What if my mom and my friends had to figure out where I was? Did I leave any clues behind?"

It started to rain.

The waves were breaking closer now. The tide was rising fast. With each breaking wave it slid farther up the beach. The foam was only ten feet from the dolphin when Austin heard his name being called.

It was the unmistakable "Aus-tin" of his mother. Then he heard a chorus of voices that could only come from his friends. The water lapped closer.

"Over here!" he called out.

His friends reached him first. They hovered in a circle around the dolphin.

"Boy! You scared the living daylights out of me," said his mother as she reached him. She hugged Austin hard.

"I couldn't leave the dolphin," Austin explained. He turned around to check on the dolphin and shouted, "Oh NO! The tide is going out again!" The tide had stopped rising three feet away.

"This is the *big* 'what-if,'" he said.

"DIG!" Austin shouted.

"What?" his mom said.

"You'll see. I have the whole process worked out in my head," Austin assured her. "First we have to dig a canal!" They all fell to their knees and dug like dogs with sand flying in all directions. The ditch was filling with water.

"Mom, would you talk to the dolphin?" Austin's mom looked puzzled for a minute, then she knelt next to the dolphin and Austin could hear her murmuring to it.

The boys dug a canal right down to the water. Marco kept out the sand that the waves dumped in, then the others went to work widening the hole around the dolphin. It was like digging a gigantic moat for a sand castle.

The boys were digging so hard, they didn't see the crowd of people gather.

"Quick! Turn him, then we can push him out!" cried Austin. He sounded desperate.

Austin held the dolphin's head while the boys crouched down and tried to push. Their feet dug into the sand, but the dolphin didn't move. Then one man came out of the crowd and knelt down as two others came forward.

The dolphin slid around and splashed in the shallow canal. Austin tried to keep its nose pointing toward the ocean. The canal was full of people, all lifting and pushing.

A big wave broke, sending water roaring up the canal. The dolphin shot forward, and the boys fell backward into the water. Camera flashes went off as the crowd cheered.

Austin struggled to his feet and watched the dolphin swim steadily toward the open sea. The adults staggered out of the water, everyone grinning. The boys stayed in the canal splashing and whooping until Austin's mom finally said, "Boys, let's do a head count. Are we all here?" They were.

That Sunday, the boys had a picnic near the spot where Austin's dolphin had come ashore. As they walked along the beach, Marco said, "What if he comes back?"

"He won't," Austin said. "Do you remember when I was holding his head just before he got free?" They all nodded. "I told him he shouldn't come ashore to meet me again. I said we'd come out to meet him, and I'll bet we do someday."